The Herb Garden

from the Poems of Bartholomew the Englishman

ESSENTIAL POETS SERIES 253

Canada Council
for the Arts

Conseil des Arts
du Canada

ONTARIO ARTS COUNCIL
CONSEIL DES ARTS DE L'ONTARIO

an Ontario government agency
un organisme du gouvernement de l'Ont

Canadä

Guernica Editions Inc. acknowledges the support of the Canada Council
for the Arts and the Ontario Arts Council. The Ontario Arts Council
is an agency of the Government of Ontario.

We acknowledge the financial support of the Government of Canada.

David Solway

The Herb Garden

from the Poems of Bartholomew the Englishman

GUERNICA
EDITIONS

TORONTO – BUFFALO – LANCASTER (U.K.)
2018

Michael Mirolla, editor
Cover design and interior layout: Errol Richardson
Guernica Editions Inc.
1569 Heritage Way, Oakville, (ON), Canada L6M 2Z7
2250 Military Road, Tonawanda, N.Y. 14150-6000 U.S.A.
www.guernicaeditions.com

Distributors:
University of Toronto Press Distribution,
5201 Dufferin Street, Toronto (ON), Canada M3H 5T8
Gazelle Book Services, White Cross Mills
High Town, Lancaster LA1 4XS U.K.

First edition.
Printed in Canada.

Legal Deposit – First Quarter
Library of Congress Catalog Card Number: 2017960336
Library and Archives Canada Cataloguing in Publication
Solway, David, 1941-, author
The herb garden : from the poems of Bartholomew the
Englishman / David Solway.

(Essential poets series ; 253)
Poems.
ISBN 978-1-77183-275-5 (softcover)

I. Title. II. Series: Essential poets series ; 253

PS8537.O4H47 2018   C811'.54   C2017-907292-7

for Asa Boxer, Max Layton and Seymour Mayne
poets, friends

... all the pleasures
of fulfillment there, a longing that is
ever realized, the loveliness of the familiar,
the alphabet of friendship learned again,
not loneliness but only the garden's green,
where all the exiles find their homes again.
—Eric Ormsby

Introductory Note

BARTHOLOMEW THE ENGLISHMAN was a 13th century Franciscan friar and scholar whose only surviving work, *De proprietatibus rerum (The Properties of Things)*, was intended as an encyclopedia of the world. I have culled certain details from the tome and added many others to construct what I conceive his garden might have been like, assuming he had one, and how he might have described it. I have also repositioned him as a poet. This collection is to be understood as an invention.

Bartholomew's system of nominal capitalization is not consistent throughout. Many of his plant names (e.g., Lesser Celandine, Valerian, Zanzibar) regularly appear in the initial upper case; others (e.g., raspberry, oregano) in the lower case. I imagined that in the prior instance Bartholomew would have considered the plants and herbs as aristocratic entities demanding proper names, and in the second as too commonplace to figure in an almanac of privilege. This is obviously a social distinction peculiar to his era, but it must also be said that Bartholomew as an herbalist and poet would have held all his plants in equal esteem. A sparse handful of the plants treated in this volume are not commonly regarded as herbs, but flourish regardless within the borders of Bartholomew's fictive garden.

As I wrote in the identically titled *The Properties of Things* (Biblioasis, 2007), the first installment in an ongoing oeuvre of which this is the second of three, "his language is a peculiar hybrid of middle and modern English, with the emphasis falling mainly on the latter to ensure comprehensibility."

The mixed dialect of the book is not intended as a *hapax legomenon* or mere linguistic gimmick, but as an effort to refresh one's poetic language as well as to study the multiple resources that the English language offers its poets as they continue to explore their craft.

Table of Contents

Proem

I salute with libations the high priest Imhotep
whose skill in healing preserved a dynasty
and attend the god Thoth whose right hand
was braceleted by a snake.
I acknowledge Ashurbanipal, King of the Assyrians,
whose tablets flourish with knowledge of herbs and plants
and the names of herbs and plants:
Apricot, Saffron, Cumin, Almond,
Mandrake, Mulberry and Turmeric.
I revere Aesculapius, son of Apollo and Coronis,
slain by a jealous god,
though some say he was born in Memphis
and his spirit diffused in gardens and parks,
father of wandering green men and women,
of rhizomotists and pharmacopolists
who continue to bustle and thrive in our markets.
I serve Hippocrates and swear by his oath,
by Apollo and Hygieia and her sister Panacea
and by all the gods and goddesses
to the best of my power of judgment.
I honour Diocles Carystius
who kindled vision with candleberry
and mapped the affinities of myrtle,
and Theophrastus to whom the Stagyrite bequeathed
his physic plots and gardens
and treatises in which are duly recorded
the properties and uses of five hundred plants.
I have studied in the School of Alexandria
and learned at the feet of celebrated mentors,
of Herophalus, Mantias, Andreas of Karystos and Apollonius Mys

and of Nikander who listed the poisons and their antidotes.
I have laboured in the court of Mithridates
and conversed with the root-gatherer Kraetus
who limned the flower down to its roots.
I have read Dioscorides
and from his *Materia Medica* have gleaned
the virtues of Cinnamon, Rhubarb, Penny, Ginger and Thyme.
I am in debt to the reverend Pliny
and to Paracelsus for the Doctrine of Signatures
and to Galen for his herbal *De Simplicibus*
and to the nameless scribes in their cloisters
who flickered like tapers in the darkness of centuries.
I have visited the libraries of Cairo and Damascus
(though sedentary in my little study)
and perused the scriptals of our saviour Avicenna
and the tracts of Abulcasis of Cordoba.
And much have I profited from the *Leech Book of Bald*
and the wisdom of Cild in simpling
and also Matthaeus Platearius and Arnold the Catalan
whose compilations illumine the darkness of earth
with experiment and observation.
And I have conned from the poem *Lacnunga* with its nine sacred
        herbs,
chiefly Waybroad which, plucked before sunrise,
untouched by iron, and bound to the head with a ribbon,
cures the headache of late lucubrations.
And from Constantine the African and Cluniac Raymond,
beloved masters of my long apprenticeship,
I have imbibed the art of sweet cultivation
equally of herbs and the mind.
And thus is the darkness of the time dispelled
by the light of scholarship
and the lamps that are lit in the depths.

Solomon's Seal

Solomon's Seal has a stout, white, creeping rhizome
twisted and knotted with circular scars,
and ribbed oval leaves that cling to the stem
like shipwrecked sailors to spars.
It shows creamy flowers drooping from the axils
but later is nubbined with berries
as blue and black as the grape
for it springs into life with allegiance.
The flowers when powdered are taken as snuff
to induce sneezing and merriment of feature
and when dissolved in water and distilled into essence
they are a staple of Italian women
renowned for the beauty of complexion.
Infusions of the root macerated in brandy
knit the bones wonderfully and make them harder
and anneal the fissures in the mouths of those
made indignant by injustice
who break their teeth with grinding.
Pounded into starch it is baked into bread
to stock the larders of the poor
in times of famine and pillage.
Yet the name is a mystery still
for some believe it arises
from likeness of the scars to impressions of a seal
and others say that it comes from its efficacy
in sealing up of wounds.
But Brother Gerard of Santa Maria
maintains when the root is cut transversely
it resembles Hebrew characters
for assembling into runes and incantations

as once the wisdom of Solomon ordained
to parry affliction of the stars
and repeal inevitability.
For although it cannot prevent disaster
it may yet exempt from its consequences.

Feverfew

Feverfew abhors confinement
and is eager to escape from gardens
and grows in walls and rocky scarps
and runs in undulant rugs out of beds and terraces.
It is a paramount analeptic.
When the leaves are cooked
they impart a bitter flavour
and drive the fever from the suffering body
with rancour and haste,
and I have read in Theologos
there is no more efficacious remedy
to deliver ambrosial sanctuary
by force, as it were, of opposites,
so that if the sick man eats
one to four fresh leaves daily
he forgets his suffering
and is able to read without distraction.
But if the roots are chopped
into a comfit of honey and fig
or boiled in sugar and water to make a syrup
the bitterness is routed but the effect is less.
This a law of all existence.
Feverfew resembles the common daisy
but is readily distinguished by its leafy bush
and recuperates desolation by tenacity and flight
because it is an eloping plant
that beckons the bound and sedentary mind
to speed in asylum over wastelands.

Foxglove

Foxglove lives in light-flecked woody dells
and reaches as high as a man,
bearing many purple flowers
which hang like upturned thimbles from the stem.
Its name is an emendation from Folksglove
because it is like the glove of the good folk or fairies
but its other names betoken caution,
as Witches Glove, Bloody Fingers and Dead Men's Balls.
In the account of Doctor Withering it is held
as a treatment for weak beating of the heart
or lutulent slowing of the blood.
It quells the fit brought on by remorse
and dispels visionary forebodings in a dram
so is a help to multitudes, multitudes
who linger in the valley of indecision.
It is beloved of bees and smaller insects
who revel in immunities
but it must not be administered injudiciously
for then it causes death on the instant
and is indeed a toxin favoured of the infidels.
Thus it is for men an instructive herb
that tells the vandal who trundles among flowers:
be tremulous and circumspect
and ginger in hankerings
for expulsion is a property of gardens.

Lemon Balm

Lemon balm is sweet-scented and perennial
and redeems waste places
from salt coast to barren plain to glabrous precipice.
It has a short rhizome,
its leaves are veiny and heart-shaped
with toothy margins,
and when it is crushed or bruised
a strong lemony aroma emanates therefrom.
The flowers are white and yellow and pink
and are called *melissa*
for their sweetness to the nostril
as well as pleasure to the eye.
Lemon Balm is the abbot's favourite
being *sine qua non* and cardinal
in all monastic apothecary gardens
where it is lovingly tended and trimmed,
and it is recommended
by Avicenna and Paracelsus
to gladden the heart and revive the spirits.
Lemon Balm has soothing and sedative properties
ingredient in herbal teas
to further sleep and good digestion
and consolation from trial.
It is a cordial against cramp and palpitation and vertigo
and cools ammoniac burnings
and protects the brain from stimulus in excess
as the body from abrasions
and is said to promote longevity.
It is used in perfumes and liqueurs
and makes an excellent marinade for fish

and a hint of lemon balm candies
jams and jellies and custards with savour;
it is also carried about in small vials
to invigorate the senses with sniffing.
When mixed with basil, hyssop and mint
and tinctured with angelica root
and stored for a year in a cask of white wine
and poured into flasks
to provision our pilgrimage
it is better than a grandmother's secret
for cheering lugubrious temper
or calming the maddened part of the mind
or for flavouring manly resilience.
For Lemon Balm is redemptive in all its properties.

𝔐𝔬𝔫𝔨𝔰𝔥𝔬𝔬𝔡

Poisonous and caustic and hardy,
Monkshood is found pushing up in clumps
on shady stream banks, ditches, pastures and high mountain
        meadows.
It has a fleshy, spindle-shaped tap-root
which resembles a little turnip
and engenders daughters every year without fail.
The stem is erect and green,
minutely downy, and grows becomingly tall
with leaves that are glossy and dark
but linen white beneath
like ladies in their camisoles.
The flowers are robed in porphyry and clerical hues
and are lovely and accessible to bees
who fuss and burrow within without peril.
It is also called *aconite* from Greek *akontion*
which is a dart
because barbarian tribes poisoned their arrows with it
though others say it comes from *akone*
which is cliffy or rocky
because that is where Monkshood sojourns and thrives.
But Pliny thinks it derives from *Aconae*
which is its place of origin.
It likes moist, loamy, penumbral soil
and grows either from the seed
or by division of the root in Autumn.
A brine of Monkshood sparged in vinegar
produces Euphorbia Polygonifolia
which dismisses warts like treacherous retainers.
And when it is washed and trimmed and dried

and stored in dark jars without air
it may be used as a balm for rheumatic pains
and as a remedy for coughs and diseases of the larynx
but should not be mingled with culinary herbs.
For Monkshood is a pharmakon of great potency
and is like a book of sorceries and spells
which must be read with cautionary eyes
or with Franciscan diffidence.
But when approached with circumspection
it teaches us vigilance and respect before the world,
working by paradox and discrepancy
in scruples fittingly apportioned
to do us good by its harmfulness.

Woad

Woad has a stout taproot and a mazy, brachiating stock
bearing rosettes in the first season
and leafy flowering shoots in the second
which are succeeded by tongue-shaped seed heads.
From its fermented leaves a dye is extracted.
(Caesar during his visit found
the natives stained and daubed with Woad
and for this reason we import it now.)
It forms the basis of indigo and black ink
but also serves as a pledget for ulcers
and a plaster for the spleen.
Bertwald the Antiquarian in his *Almanack* affirms:
"A plaister made thereof and applied to the left side
takes away the hardness and the pain thereof
as it drains fretting and corroding humours
and cools the fever of infection."
Those who are left-sided and fond of paints
are therefore extravagantly partial to Woad,
yet even those who lean to sobriety
and martial their letters from the right
(as did Caesar who despoiled the island of the herb)
acknowledge the tincture of Woad in reflection,
in curative virtue, and as a lusty endowment
in the conquest of the febrile and the subfusc.

Vervain

Vervain grows in wild waste shires,
along roadsides, in moors, and among ruined buildings
but is not the less for indigence or desuetude
because it is tough and sinewy.
Its leaves are lobed and notched
consorting in pairs like lovers or friends
or sibilant conspirators against tyranny,
and the flowers small and mauve
are arranged in long slender spikes at the finial.
"Vervain" is derived from our Celtic forbears
who say *ferfaen*, that is,
to drive away the stone,
as it is druidic against pains of the bladder,
breaking up the calculus with dispatch.
And it is also a great aphrodisiac
called by the Latins *Herba veneris*
for whetting concupiscence and spurring the flesh
and so is beloved of the ribald and profligate.
It is a strong protection against dementia
and a physic against jaundice and toothache
and according to the sage and venerable Culpeper
it remedies the cold distempers of the womb
and is a charm against wicked and furtive spirits.
And Culpeper has also affirmed with authority
from the study of ancient manuscripts
Vervain was found on the Mount of Calvary
and staunched the wounds of the crucified Christ
wherefore it is said to confer immortality.
Gather the leaves before the flowers ripen fully
and prepare in seasonable decoctions.

Southernwood

The leaves of Southernwood have a tart lemony taste
and are used to flavour pies in France and Italy
and crullers among the Dutch.
It restores balance to the visceral flora.
According to renowned apothecaries
it is why Germans can gorge without sickness
which accounts for its other name "Old Warrior."
It is an abortifacient, emmenagogue, tonic and astringent
and repels tiredness in the field.
Spaniards mingle it with camomile
which they call Manzanilla as they do with Sherry
to lighten the gloom of Toledo
while the sons of Albion sprinkle
a pulver of Southernwood on crumpets and buns
to spice insipid collocations.
It is rarely found in the wild
but is cut, notched and grafted in gardens
and blended in a commonwealth of influences
like the products of the workshop and the study.
I keep a sprig of Southernwood in my secretary drawer
and consult it regularly during composition.

Onion

Onions are strong-smelling and domey
and have a bulbous root with many layers of flesh
apparelled in white, yellow and purple tunics
from which shoot tall hollow stems,
and the leaves are channelled and ridged
and numerous celadon flowers adorn the top of the stems.
Onions are antiseptic, antibiotic, antisclerotic, diuretic and
        expectorant,
reduce the pressure of the blood,
heal wounds, absolve the vitals, and subdue colds,
are eaten to ward off phlebitis
and applied as a compress to allay insect stings and migraines.
Onions are propagated in sets
well-sheltered under trees and makeshift trellises
for they shrivel in too much sun
and are lashed and molested by wind.
Onions are native to the Holy Land
but have spread like the gospels to the world
growing in every vegetable garden
to offer reprieve and exemption against forgetfulness
for they are like fish transmuted to earth,
rich in phosphor and scaled with glistenings.
Rooted in symbol,
they urticate the memory
and jolt and startle thought into being
by reeking in their clamps
for they are teasing and pungent as parables.

Comfrey

Comfrey is good for healing of bones
which its other names attest
as Knitbone, Boneset and Bruisewort,
and is well reputed as a vulnerary.
Make a compress from the grated root
imbrued with water and mud
and clench it tightly to the afflicted part:
as if by magic segment is united to segment.
It is also an exemplary compost
and gardeners lay it on the bottom of a trench when planting
to help in quick decomposition.
Learn, my sons, from the doubleness of Comfrey
when meted out seasonably and with prudence
as quintessence of the appropriate.
For Comfrey links what is broken
yet dissolves what is massed together.

Peony

Peony thickens among pine,
cedar and hornbeam oak and among bracken
in the north of rocky limestone slopes
and along the edges of profitable cultivation.
Peony gems in narrow segments and gleaming carpels
and often shows pubescent follicles,
summoning memories of childhood gardens
consecrated to no purpose but joy.
For I have read in the Heretics
that nothing is more useful than beauty.
Mine is called *Rubra Plena* for its double-deep red,
proliferating early
along the borders of the herb garden
in vast colonies of unmeasured ravishment.
I love it for its *belle poitrine*
(so called by Jean Palaiseul in his reveries)
clefting in amplitudes from its beds and its bodices.
And although I am an herbalist in essence
and wary by vocation
of the weaving of idle flowers
in tapestries to be hung against the cold,
I am enamoured of marigold and rose
which are profitless to infirmity
and cultivate peony as a sacrament to the world.
For it causes the senses to falter and swoon,
heavening the air
with odour of nut and orient spice.
And it has no use but beauty.

𝕷𝖚𝖓𝖌𝖜𝖔𝖗𝖙

Lungwort grows in damp woods and hedgerows
with a bunchy corpulent root,
a hairy stem that towers over grasses
and clusters of pink flowers
shaped like a little bell
(or the bone in the small of the back
where it is nestled and wedged),
smalting at the end of the stems
and blooming from March to May in riotous teeming.
It is called Lungwort
from the Doctrine of Signatures
which holds that plants resemble what they treat
for it is powerful against
consumption of the lungs and bronchial clogging.
It is also called Soldiers and Sailors
for it is an antidote by grinding down
and by soaking of leaves to make them palatable
against omens and apprehensions.
In some the leaves are long and narrow
with white spots and vivid blue edges
but in others violet and red,
the flowers rising neatly in crossed racks,
the space in between a gleaming hiatus
for the passage of flickering things.
But however pleasing to the sense
and affable to daintiness,
when the root is powdered and mixed with water
it reduces inflammations and scalds
and the stem is a most wonderful compost
that aids decomposition of plants

fresh in the bottom of a trench.
And this confirms by the Doctrine of Antinomies
that grace and comeliness
are sturdy against evil
and that beauty is also serviceable to man.

Zanzibar

Zanzibar is the root of an herb
which is cold and wet,
yet has a wild and sharp savour
beloved of poets and philosophers
as is said in Platearius.
It is a help against evils
of the breast and the lungs
and eases the ache of stomach and guts,
putting out easily all windy ventosities
and thus is beloved of theologians.
The more white it is and younger
the sharper it is and better
but if left too long to moulder in cellar
it is forwhirled with worms
and rots of the moisture within.
Therefore to keep Zanzibar a long while
it is best to domicile it among peppers
that the moisture of Zanzibar
may be appeased by the dryness of the pepper.
The same is true of Juniper
which harshens Zanzibar for continuance.
From the properties of Zanzibar
as has been said by many
did the emperors of China reign nigh immortal
but this Bartholomew does not credit
save as a gassy exhalation
clouding the ventricles of the brain
in sedentary or deluded travellers.
But it is good in medicines applied from without
for medlied with brimstone and vinegar

it reduces swellings
and mollifies the bite of the addercop,
and pulvered with seed, rind and root
it scours festering wounds.
Isaac and Abulafia say
that when it is medlied with barley meal
and powder of saffron
and daubed along the lower belly
it helps conception and birth in women
as it does when brayed on the brow of men
who bring forth progeny from Zanzibar.

Rue

It is found on dry rocky slopes and limestone screes
with a ligneous root and a branching stem,
stalked leaves in alternates
bluish-green and lobed like an ear,
and the flowers which are greenish-yellow
are flared like little trumpets or funnels.
It is named from Greek *reuo*, to set free,
for it releases the body from the fetters of infirmity.
It is also called Herb of Grace
for holy water is sprinkled from brushes of rue
to manumit the spirit from corruption.
It is useful in incantations against witches and strangers,
is a factor of taste in stinging liquors
which dissipate the bolus and pacify the cramp,
and makes a brackish tea potent against the nausea.
The leaves are chewed to refresh the mouth
and when coupled with wormwood and vigorously rubbed
it chases the stench of plague to purify rooms,
being thus a requisite in every pharmacopoeia.
For without Rue is ruefulness and dismay
for Rue is a necessary element by transposition in character
to face the time as it were with tartness
and with humour both bitter and keen.

℮regano

Oregano sprouts in hedge banks and in scrub.
It favours dry chalky ground,
rising in delicate fonts of rose-lilac buds
to the height of a small child.
It comes from Greek *oros* which means mountain
and *ganos* which means joy
for it brings joy on mountain sides
where satyrs disport with lissome maids
and it crowns young couples in marriage.
Clipped to the belt in lavender bags
it is coveted by Germans in their caves
and it is also planted on graves
for it brings joy even to the dead.
It is a superior tonic and diuretic
rebuking dyspepsia and regimenting menarche
and is a cure for thrush and other infections
and when steeped for a time in cotton wool
it relieves the hay fever.

Jean Palaiseul in his tractate
intricately reasoned and authoritative
advises simmering oregano in lard in a bain-marie
with the horn of a unicorn well pounded
before straining and bottling
as a vade mecum to accompany the Bible
on a preacher's travels.
In concert with the Holy Book
this produces vision and understanding
but also sharpens the gusto,
instructs the palate,

converts the stomach to lickerish contentment
and makes of a lean philosopher
or a dry theologian
a most congenial trencher mate.
For as the learned Sorbonnite asserts
in his treatise on oregano
man does not live by spirit alone.

Lesser Celandine

Blooming toward the end of winter
Lesser Celandine is the poet's herb
for it is lovely and bright
and its flowers grow single and whole,
enduring each its own vicissitude.
The leaves of the stalk are fibrous and dark
but the lower leaves sheathing the stem
form a rosette to ravish the eye,
and it is often to be found
chiselled on tombstones for remembrance
in few-flowered bracted spikes.
It has a preference for marshes and swamps
and thus is esteemed of the frog
and other homely creatures
who live hidden and inconspicuous,
and by its other name of Pilewort
it is known as a cure for the emerod
and is a favourite of practical herbalists.
It is anodyne against varicose veins
and other hard wens and tumours
but rubbed excessively against the skin
it induces sores and ulcers
even the leaves of the Mullein may not counter.
And in all these degrees and qualities
Lesser Celandine is heraldic of the poet
whose words are spice and ointment in May
but in February chafe and discomfit,
who blossoms late in the cycle of time
and who flourishes individual among multitudes.

Valerian

Valerian springs from many bundles of hollow roots
like grooved hollow stems lashed together.
The leaves are bright green and lanciform
and the flowers crowd like cherubs on the stalk
redolent of nard.
Its common name is All Heal
for it is applied to many purposes
as in leeching by our forefathers
or by Fabius Calumna against the falling sickness
for he cured himself with an extract.
It is also prescribed for vertigo, sleeplessness and St. Vitus' Dance.
A rich constituent in spices, scents and ointments
it is laid among clothes for fragrance
but also capillary mats for its texture.
If you put Valerian roots in your pockets
it will attract rats irresistibly to their ruin
by plunging off cliffs and in rivers where you lead them.
Mixed with licorice, raisins and aniseed
it clears the lungs and facilitates breathing
and drives wind from the belly
and sneaps splinters and thorns from the flesh.
Because it will grow in any soil
it is thus a text for homilies as well
for Valerian is ubiquitous yet precious as sard
and rare because it is common.

Ground Elder

Ground Elder is a rampant and persistent weed in gardens
as well as in ecclesiastical rubble.
It produces a cloying odour when rubbed
and has a creeping root system
that smothers other plants in snags and snarls.
Its stiff biretta flowers serve
as forage for wild beasts
and its seeds are devoured by magpies and crows
to make them querulous and cheeky.
It was in olden times called Goatspod
from Greek *aigos*, goat, and *podos*, foot,
and when this was kneaded with Latin *podagra*, gout,
in lexical confection which is the bread and confiture of scholars
it came to be known as Goatweed
which is its other name.
But by whichever name it is known
it is a pestilent plant notwithstanding
that relishes complexity of roots and sources
as in the needless wrangle of the senescent
grubbing for relics and origins
in sweet corruption of embroilment.
Therefore it is most advisable
never to introduce it into your garden.

Marigold

Marigold likes temperate climes,
its numberless tufts bedecking
the banks of mountain brooks and streams
in vast profusions of gold.
The leaves are shaped as kidneys
growing from a spongy stem
at first most unprepossessing,
but when the flowers and sepals are heaped uncountably
like coins spilling over
from the rims of their leafy green goblets
it is sacred to the Virgin in festivals.
Ah! but then it is woven into garlands for brides
who celebrate Spring
with the gift of their bodies
for Marigold betokens bountiful days
and prodigal daughters unstinting and exorbitant
who consummate morning with evening and night,
with loves, and with babes abounding.

Dill

Dill is the *anethon* of Dioscorides
mentioned in the papyrus of the Egyptians
as a potent carminative and remedy for flatulence
by continual gusty expulsions,
thus exhausting the tempest in the gut.
Yet it is belied by its delicacy of form.
For it has a striped and slender stem,
beryl-blue plumage of leaves
similar to fennel and caraway but more luxuriant,
a nexus of yellow flowers,
an inrolled intricate complexity of petals,
and thin ridged wales in the fruit,
all of which mantle the garden
in a gossamer tracery of rundles and sprigs.
Yet it is a robust component
in the gripe water of infants
when macerated raw with kale and cucumber
and liberally salted in a draught.
For as happens often in the world,
confuting manifestation
however beneficial in the outcome,
the effect mistenders the visible embodiment.

Rose

Among all the flowers of the world
the rose is best and bears the prize
for by fairness it feeds the eyes
and pleases the nose by odour
and the touch by soft handling
(when the thorn is duly lopped or plucked)
and the taste by sugar of the hips
and the ear by wind harping though its bundles.

The rose is also medicinable
in flower, branch and seed,
banishing headache by its plaited leaves
or curing the colic with tisane and poult.
But if it is not forgendered and shorn
it goes out of kind to become a wild rose
which veers to early whiteness soon to be dismantled
by excessive spending of its substance.
But the houseled rose has many clustered leaves
more red than white
and frolics in great assemblies,
wafting a sweet fragrance to the nostril of the sceptic
to convince him otherwise.

Still it is painful to the mind and heart.
For the young rose shoots from a green knap;
then from a spray of tender leaves
and a clutch of delicate twigs and reedy tendrils and stems
and seeds that cleave to the fruit,
it spreads itself against the sun rising
until it is ripe and red.

But when leaf and petal come to the brink of harvest
it grows first hectic,
next pale and ghostly and stale as an unwed maid,
turns black about winter time
when it is ferried in bunches in the storm's tumbrels
to bleakness and despair.
So the rose flourishes chiefly in memory.

All this happens in a season quickly
whether it springs from seed or setting or grafting
or from any manner of tending.
It is therefore an emblem of all sensibility
and a sad epitome of our works and days
that blossom mostly in reminiscence.

Purple Loosestrife

Purple loosestrife is a duple and codified plant.
Its name is *Inthron*, or noble,
alluding to the royal pigment of the flowers,
but its other name is *Salix*, willow,
since it likes to grow under willows beside water
where it is everywhere to be seen,
its leaves approximating to the grey sallow
which is not received with approbation.
For this reason Purple Loosestrife
is a type and figure of attenuated things,
misrepresented in all modern herbaries
which neglect and misprize the legacy of the ancients
which men can no longer decipher or possess.
For although it was treasured by herbalists of old
it is today disregarded and contemned
as a plant of little value.
But as John Paul August the poet has written
this, like the commonplace, is an error of perception.
For it is a striking addition to gardens.

Marsh Mallow

Marsh Mallow is pretty and decorative
with a long, tough, fleshy, whitish and tapering root,
a tall velvety stem
and delicately cupped incarnadine flowers
followed by round flat fruit called "cheeses."
Antonio of Musa in his tractate on herbs
says it will cure forty seven odd diseases,
and Catullus says it is a great panacea
to cool and dry and comfort the member,
and Horace in his Odes proclaims
it is a choice depilatory
for all who are dug barbarously deep in hair
or are beardsly in appearance.
It is a godsend to Armenians
who subsist on Marsh Mallow when cultivation fails
as it does most often in that dolorous land
and in Gaul the young tops and leaves
are eaten raw to stimulate the loins
for the Gauls are much given to venery.
But among the English who preen on discernment
the mallow is specific for adversity in love
and disillusion and distress when friendship falters
for when steeped in cold water and strained and heated
and quaffed without let or intermission
it braces the spirit against betrayal by friends
which occurs in England as often and bitterly
as flagging of intention among the Gauls
or failure of crops in Armenia.

Rape Seed and Olive

Of rape seed and the fruit of the olive
is oil made
and it has many uses,
but chiefly in lamps
and mortars of candlesticks
as in the temple of Jerusalem.
For it is said in Exodus
it is good and appropriate to offer oil,
not of mulberry and myrtle
but of the olive tree and of rape seed.
For it is not lawful to offer
any other oil
as it is not lawful to revere
any fire but that
which comes down from heaven
to kindle in the flicker of observance.
And therefore be intent
that your offering is acceptable
and that your oil
be of olive or rape seed
but not of mulberry or myrtle.
For in small discriminations lies salvation
and from the wick of a little thing
flares the light of perfection
and all celestial recompense.

Mandrake

Mandrake is related to an edible tuber.
It has a large, brown, parsnippy root
with brawny divided tangs
that plunge deep into the ground
like a troll to its mother
and grows plentifully under the murderer's gallows
and on grave mounds where it flourishes mightily.
The fruit are small and round like green tomatoes
but turn an opulent yellow when ripe
and are aromatic as the pine apple.
It is always inscribed in the ancient lists
of magical and medicinal herbs
where it is known as Satan's Apple
whose office is to free from possession by demons
and therefore it is often compacted into amulets.
Yet it is related to an edible tuber.
Pliny says the root was chewed before cutting the flesh
for its lenitive and insensitive properties
and it is written in the tomes of the scholiasts
that the sponge given to Christ
was dipped in an elixir of Mandrake
and also that Mandrake brings good fortune
in healing sterility of the soul.
And yet it is related to an edible tuber.
The juice expressed from the grated root
relieves scrofulous tumours and convulsions
and is an admirable molinist drug and medicament
against sadness and mania and delirium.
But it is chary of picking and difficult
to acquire for planting in gardens

for it is shy and elusive as a spirit to be summoned.
And yet it is related to an edible tuber.

St John's Wort

St John's Wort delivers itself kindly
in grasslands, open woods and clearings
indifferent to most desolations.
It has a stumpy rhizome and crooked stems
woody at the bottom and forked at the top,
the leaves are stippled with translucent dots
and the petals grow like the fingers of the hand
for it is a strange and wonderful herb.
St John's Wort yields a red oil
that is favoured by crusaders
for redemption of slashes and wounds
and is estimable against catarrh and inflammations
and induces euphoria in the melancholy.
To make the oil
grind the flowers and leaves
in a glass cruet or jar
and cover with a muslin against flies
(as a book must be sealed from the firebrat)
and stand the cruet or jar
in the blessedness of the sun
for about three weeks or four
until the oil turns a deep good red
to be rubbed on gashes and sprains.
St John's Wort flourishes in any kind of soil,
some sun, some shade,
and responds like the Baptist with resilience
to any calamity that befalls.
Cherish it.

Carline Thistle

The Carline Thistle is the plant
on which the angel's arrow lighted
as a sign to the Emperor Charlemagne
that this would mend his army of the pestilence,
which is how we derive its name.
But whether or no the legend is accepted
it is good against disorders of the skin
and is the only thing for the qualm
(as Cardinal Benedictus declares in his text)
and its miniature suns illumine the quotidian
as in sere and abandoned tracts;
also waters distilled from the Carline Thistle
will make us see the commonplace anew
and acquit and commute from the plague of custom
which is a most dire blight.
It has many small uses but significant
for it is applied as a rustic barometer
which expands in dessicate weather
but closes when rain is imminent:
thus it enlightens by diminutive intimacies,
and like centaury and wormwood
it is a grateful treatment for shingles,
and it is also used in dry bouquets and everlastings
for it retains its scent and appearance for ever.
The flowers are gathered into crowns
with an aureate center
and surrounded by silvery radiating bracts.

Deadly Nightshade

Deadly Nightshade grows in shady parts
of woods and thickets and shrubs,
near old abbeys and ruins on chalky soil
and also in the garden of Atropos
who cuts the thread of life
for it is a most deadly and unforgiving plant.
Yet it is known as *bella donna*
for Italian women squeeze the juice in their eyes
to make them shine brightly and alluringly
and draw men to their immediate undoing
envenomed by beauty and the luminous glance.
It is also known as *dwale*
which is Old Norse for death and sleep
for it is a mortal and unrelenting plant
which is conveyed by its other names:
Devil's Berries, Laureate's Curse, Naughty Man's Cherries and
          Dreaded Sibyl.
Marcus Antoninus had occasion to regret
the lethal properties of this herb
which reduced his maniples in Parthia,
and the Scot more recently subdued the Dane
by mixing it into the peace cup.
And yet it is a beneficial plant
if used in moderation and respected
for Friar Juniper has diligently shown
in his learned commentary on the *lusus naturae*
that tiny doses of belladonna tincture
protect from scarlet fever,
and like its brothers Thornapple and Bittersweet
when its leaves are smoked and taken in

it allays the whooping cough and bladder spasm,
and in pastes and plasters it soothes piles and abscesses,
and is a gift of God for constipation;
further, as a restorative tonic for the syphilis
it is nonpareil
in curing its melancholy consequences.
For it is an alkaline and sacerdotal plant
numinous in all its properties.

Sweet Woodruff

Sweet Woodruff flourishes in woody places with dappled light.
It is equally known as Master of the Wood
and steeped in claret
makes a delightful drink called Maybowl.
Father Loewenfeld the Benedictine
who is a great lover of the Maybowl
advises soaking Sweet Woodruff in a large ewer
of lemon juice, sugar and cold wine
with strawberries dimpling the tautened skin,
and this is therapeutic
for dour and lugubrious men
who linger too long in scriptorium.
It gives off a giddy aroma of hay and vanilla
when used for strewing in churches
to affront the demon with benignity
and if put in among linen wards off the moth.
It is rich in fragrant coumarin
to garnish potpourris and fancy snuffs
and perfumes the provocative ladies of the town
who multiply now like the generations
of finches and chickadees and lightheaded birds,
filling the air with their scattersong
and distracting palladian men by a secondary effect
to repel the gloominess of the time.
And this Bartholomew approves in whatever form
for the world has grown dark and heavy with travail.

Watercress

Watercress is commonly found
in shallow slow water in rivers and sluices and wetlands
where it is fished for the kitchen as it were
by tugging and plucking
and sometimes by scooping with nets.
Its other name is Nasturtium
which comes from Latin *nasus tortus*
or "writhing nose"
for it is pungent to excess.
Watercress is mentioned by Dioscorides
in his *Materia medica*
in the first century of the year of our Lord
(and a Fifth Gospel for loyal herbalists)
as a most flemishing aphrodisiac soup
and an aid to recovery of appetite
in sallow and stringy ascetics
who return from the wilderness
in renunciation and despair.
And it also fecundates the scalp
better than oil of laurel
for abundant harvest of hair
and scours the complexion of freckles and blemishes
and brings down swelling of the glands.
The venerable Culpeper recommends
a poultice of watercress for disorders of the lymph,
for chilblains and roseola
and virulent ulcers of the privy parts,
but care must be taken in picking
(and in this is Culpeper both stern and insistent)
since dissemination of the liver-fluke

in sheep that graze near water
is a danger to be avoided
more by vigilance than by presentiment.
For attention is the highest form of prayer.
And in purveying of such counsel
Culpeper is empirical before man
but also humble before the Lord
by leaving not everything to providence.

Raspberry

Raspberry is a prickly bush
that loves to grow on heaths and in improbable places.
Its leaves are plumose and brambly,
yet from a thin foam of white flowers
scanty and peaked
round red fruit ripen in Spring.
Now they must be mashed and infused with water
and once decanted and strained
and sweetened with a little honey,
gelatins, marmalades, syrups and aspics
ripen again in pots and portico cups.
When brought to becoming mothers in small bowls
so as not to offend propensity
it eases childbirth by bracing
of the reproductive muscles
and strengthens the tired sinews of the womb.
And if hulled and baked in meal
it makes a toothsome cruller in the aftermath.
Thus it is a study in unlikelihood
for out of small beginnings come
as if from the pages of an herbalist's manual
or raspberries in a dish of milk
effects unimaginable in embryo.

Tansy

Tansy has a crawling rootstock
and grows wild on meres and hilly eskers
and in mossy places near the Cornish coast.
Its leaves are viridian and ferny
and its flowers are like biscuits of shortbread.
Tansy has numerous commendable uses.
It expels worms in children
and it keeps away fleas and banebugs and ticks,
being thus the salvation of dogs.
In men it is a stimulant after Lent
when the appetite flags from discontinuance
and loss of belief in festivity.
For Tansy has a long history of the table
and the leaves are milled in omelettes and puddings
or crumbled on flitches, gammons and rashers,
for its hot peppery properties replace
nutmeg and cinnamon on a humble man's shelf.
And Tansy tea is a potion for dyspepsia
as well as a philter for indifference.
But its name discloses its principal virtue
as it comes from Greek *athanatoia*
which means immortality
as it lasts perpetually
and was given to Ganymede to make him immortal
and preserves the dead from putrefaction.
It is thus a grave and momentous canonical secret
which Bartholomew utters with some trepidation
and fear of untimely reprisal
since it causes the odour of sanctity in saints
and as one of many apostolic beguilements
sustains the faith of the credulous.

Basil

Basil does not grow in my garden
for it is what herbalists call an exotic
native to India and Persia
(as is chess which is an exotic game)
and it hates frost most passionately.
But I know of Basil from recondite texts
that its leaves are a shining green with intricate veining
and the flowers wax like moonlets in creamy whorls;
that its name derives from Greek *basileos*, or king,
to signal the esteem in which it is held;
that it is particularly good sprinkled on salads
and is tasty in stews of poultry and mushrooms;
that fresh juice from the leaves dropped in the ear
eases inflammation and conciliates deafness;
that it comes in several kindred breeds
as Sweet Basil, Purple Basil, Lemon Basil, Sacred Basil and Bush
       Basil,
all growing from seed in an herb garden
or in a window box or hanging pot;
and that although it is a most temperate herb
it may be coaxed with discipline and love
into a facsimile of hardiness.
Therefore I await the gift of seed
from travelling merchants and itinerant monks
who return from the orient with treasures.
But for the time in which I am without
like an exile in my proper garden
I console myself with texts
and the dreamy pleasures of anticipation.

Savoury

Savoury, Winter or Summer, is a relishing herb
and perennial regardless of epithet
and is gathered on rocky parapets
in joyful and convivial clusters
ascending and branching for instruction and delight.
It has a small distaff-like root
and its leaves are middle green to red with glandular spots
and is charming in rockeries and borders
as it complements the pot and the basket.
Its name is from *satyros* for it is a potent love drug
and as Cardinal Benedictus claims in his *Conspectus*:
"It is an essential ingredient in possets
for frigid and impotent couples
and thus it is an herb of happiness."
It is also known as the bean herb
for it brings out the flavour of the bean without dominating
and aids in digestion of beans
which are pre-eminent among fartibles.
And because it contains a strong and reliable volatile oil
it is vehement against fermenting intestinal flora,
companioning pork and cucumber
and neighbourly in the distillation of spirits.
Bees are also fond of Savoury
and produce a celestial honey
to comfort the fallen with sweetness.
For Savoury is an altogether jubilant herb
swarming and burgeoning in happy bunches
most like children in the primogenitive time.

Lady's Bedstraw

The small bright yellow flowers of Lady's Bedstraw
are clustered in pinnacles at the end of the stalk
to accost the passerby with steepled gleams
and tiny inklings of delight,
yet it is more than a mere allurement.
It is appropriate for many diverse things
and is good for curdling milk and renning cheese
and in Tuscany it is used for sweetening goat's cheese
but in Britain for colour and substance.
Among men who suffer for their crimes
when applied as a dressing or salve
it alleviates the chafing of manacles.
It is also an excellent stuffing for mattresses
and was the principal among cradle herbs
for the manger at Bethlehem.
For the Saviour too demanded amenity
from the maiden who bore Him to forfeiture
before entering upon His ministry and fate
to bring an end to all bodily repose.

Fumitory

Fumitory is called Earth Smoke by herbalists
because it is born of the vapours of the earth,
resembling from a distance a field on fire,
and with smoke of the burning tinder of its roots
it brings tears to the eyes to clear the sight
of those who suffer from miasma or stye.
It is most beneficial for bile and colic
and is good for fading of liver spots in elders
and cradle cap in infants.
For Fumitory is a robust and clambering plant
that encompasses both sides of life,
bracketing the continuum of misery with abatement.
Served as a tea before nightfall
and flavoured with mint or orange zest
it soothes the gums of child and greybeard,
one before teeth and the other after,
for both are sensible of what is to come
and bitterly complain of ensuings.
Thus its leaves are silver and grey
but its flowers are pink with ruddiness
to signal a double consolation
since it is both an ornament and an indispensable herb
like a tale told by the universal bard
who nurses and cultivates tranquil imaginings
in the gardens of the young and the old.

Elecampane

Elecampane grows in fields, waysides and copses
and has a plump bulging root
which is candied and eaten as a sweetmeat
resembling Cardamon in taste.
The leaves are heart-shaped and rough
but soft and felty on the underside
and the flowers mimic the heliotrope in splendour
while the fragrance is that of the violet.
But Elecampane may be cultivated from seed
and also propagated by off-cuts
from old roots in Autumn
with a bud or an eye on each,
and dibbled in a moist sunny bed well-weeded
will reward your effort with similitudes.

Its name is an allusion to Helen of Troy
for it is told that Helen in innocence and joy
was clutching a bunch of Elecampane
when snatched away by nefarious Paris,
and alternately it is said
that Elecampane bloomed from the tears she shed.
But Latin which is a pedestrian tongue
gives *inula* and *campane*, or "of the fields,"
which misleads by being prosaic.

Thus I, Bartholomew, by this set down
my love for Elecampane
which is more moving and lovely in Greek than in Latin,
knowing it is but a canny simulacrum
as Helen in Troy was a billowy shift,

and as thought is a copy of the Lord's speculation
that in Heaven governs our feigning.

Catnip

Beloved of cats and a potent aphrodisiac
catnip is a pungent perennial herb
and has branched woolly stems tall as a dwarf
for it is large in its littleness.
It is indeed a lovely and mischievous plant
growing in dense whorls on the leafy axils
with small white flowers shading to pink
and blushing in spots of hectic delectation.
Its fragrance is reminiscent of mint
which accounts for its alternate name "catmint"
from Greek *kata* "towards" and *menthe* "mint"
for it leans toward the odour of nepenthe—
though perhaps "cat" creeps into the thicket of etymology.
It is also good for children's ailments
and eases grimping, restlessness and nether pneumatics
and also smoking the leaves smothers the hiccup.
It thuribles caudles and darioles
to tickle the palate of the gastronome
howsoever devout and exacting.
But here is its greatest virtue and advantage
for as an unguent concocted from the flowering tops
in the proper season of the moon
it restores catamenial harmony in the tardy and irregular,
relieving the condition of domestic anxiety,
renewing playfulness in the home
and favouring in this way a sunny disposition
among spouses, children and cats.

Toadflax

Toadflax is busy in fields of gravelly marls,
leaping upward in dense spikes of yellow flowers
like the snapdragon but taller and more arching
and resembles eggs and butter in their platters.
In Greece it is boiled in milk
and left to stand where flies are troublesome
since toadflax is effective against winged irritations.
But its virtue is revealed by its name
as it provides shelter for toads under its vault
which is a good and blessed thing to do
for toads are a sign of fecundity and faith
whose call ferments like a malted tumult
in booming unisons of content,
filling the night with liturgical regurgitations
and fulminating mightily against emptiness.
I grow it in my cottage garden
for I am inordinately fond of toads.

Coreopsis

Bushy with short rhizomes and much-branched stems,
leaves hairy and segmented
and sometimes toothed and woolly,
thirsting for well-drained soil,
glowing yellow to pale lemon in colour,
its nine petals radiating to the heavens,
it is known as Coreopsis—
a lovely name when syllabled on the tongue
and fit for the gardens of rhetoric and tournure
as in Brother Trehane's *Index Hortensis*
where it is written as Cobham Gold
and also as Wirral Supreme.
But growing in open woods and clearings
and in somewhat dry soil,
with only seven petals to its name,
its seed resembling a bedbug in its burrowing,
it is also known as tickweed,
tough as a costrel,
tall and burly and not much celebrated.
Coreopsis is the lustre that glimmers in my revery.
Tickweed is my namesake and reverend in its rootedness.

Dittany

A small aromatic shrub and pleasantly medicinal
though green as cadaver and rimmed with shroud
and with leaves bristly as an old man's ears,
Dittany seals wounds, laves the bite of the snake, greases childbirth
and is an unrivalled remedy against
the slitherings and insurgencies of the inner coils.
With Dittany is no eructation nor diverticulum of the gut
nor sudden voidings and soilings of the breech.
It is endemic to Crete
and grows in abundance on Mount Dicte,
birthplace of the Thunderer
whose choler and vehemence were calmed by Dittany.
Dioskorides says that goats pierced with arrows
were healed by cropping of Dittany
to flee with impunity both malice and hunger
and thus did the Cretans suffer dearth of goatsflesh.
It is known as *Amaracus* dictamus in Latin
and Dictamo in Greek (written with *iota*)
but is *alexipharmic* in any language.
Dittany is the gift of friendship
and stifles the fallings-out of dyspeptic confrontations
as well as anxieties of departure.
I have none in my kitchen to soak and administer
but it flourishes exuberantly in my library
where it is potted in books
and beckons like a viaticum on the shelf.

Mountain Balm

Mountain balm grows wild
along hedgerows, roadsides, dry banks
and in waste and woody places,
erect and bushy with a creeping rootstock.
But it is also cultivated.
It cousins thymes and ground ivies
and is best when it is tended diligently.
Fra Gerard recommends it
to cure "melanchole and sorrowfulness"
and it is also excellent against convulsions of the brain
and calms afflictions of the nerves
but is most appropriate in *flagrante*.
A poultice made with a wad of leaves
and heated gently with an iron
soothes bruises and the deep purple blotch on the lower lip
caused by the bite of lupercalian lovers
who are strangers to decorum.
Mountain balm is a trumpet in the wild
but cultivated makes for a dulcet companion
to those who are given overmuch to debauchery
and live apprehensive of homecoming.

Lavender

Fragrant and therapeutic is lavender
and a haven to bees who rummage in plunder.
You may recognize it readily.
Lavender has a short ramifying stem
with countless straight, woody, quadrangular, silky, grey branches
though its opposite, stalkless, long, sagittary leaves
are pale green and shine with their own inner light
to bait and distract the eye of the cynic
who has no traffic with beauty.
The essential oil will kill a snake,
a tincture strengthens the hair and the joints
and was therefore sprinkled by the Romans in their baths
and a lotion will heal infections and burns
as it graces too the embalmer's pharmacopoeia
yet renders alert the somnolent mind.
When the flowers grow brittle
they are chipped into pouncets
and added to potpourris and oil of lavender
for soaps and emollient powders.
Thus lavender has many uses and applications
which may be culled from *Grandmother's Secrets*
and other worthy compendiums.
Prune the bush after flowering to encourage denser growth
and pluck the terminal spike
to skewer the bone of the skeptical detractor
who belittles the wisdom of the bees and the Romans
and has no time for the pleasures of the garden
or to leaf through the pages of *Grandmother's Secrets*.

Camphor

It is a huddling, aromatic, homuncular shrub
and a pretty plant to grow in an herb garden
because of its silver-grey leaves and conciliate scent.
But it also grows wild in neglected fields
and in waste grounds and calcareous soil
for it is hardy and resilient to a fault.
Its feathery lobes sport cream and yellow flowers
which bloom profusely into September
and rescue the Fall with the Summer
rivalling the Danaë rose in munificence.
Yet it is much esteemed domestically
for its stimulant and antiseptic properties
and is used to expel the intestinal worm
and to blunt the probing sting of the mosquito.
The Arabs are said to have made a salve
from its pounded and crushed lemony buttons
to knit up wounds and hasten the scar
for the Arabs are an erudite people
though much disposed to slaughter and mayhem.
Whether in the wild or the nursery
let us learn from the Arabs to heal *in extremis*
and from Camphor to live in exfoliate peace.

Mugwort

Mugwort is a vigorous spreading plant
with purplish stems branching at the zenith
and flowers that flatten in ovals.
"Mugwort" comes from ancestral *mucwyrt*,
that is, "midge" and "wort,"
for it is hostile to small winged predators
that discomfit us with nibbles;
but as *Artemisia vulgaris*, from its patroness Artemis
as an embrocation against the menopause.
Mugwort is also of hieratic bearing
for St. John the Baptist wore a girdle of mugwort
when he went into the wilderness
as a talisman to ward off malevolent spirits;
but for the common sort pitted against lesser devils
it aids digestion of fatty meats and oily fish
and for women in delivery it rids the afterbirth
by sitting over it to draw down the courses.
It is much cherished in Wales especially
for mugwort is apt for Celtic distempers:
infused in brandy it is a remedy for gout
and highly recommended for anyone named Trevor.

Clove Pink

Clove Pink embroiders the courtyard
but is sometimes found in old walls as an escape.
It is one of the earliest flowers
to be cultivated in Britain
and is prized for the decorative and the culinary
which makes it unlike the temper of an island
that otherwise knows little of the kitchen
and even less of ornamentation.
Spicy and clove-like in ales and wines,
its petals are candied to decorate cakes
and as the liqueur *ratafia*
pestled in spirits and taken one glassful a day
is most effective against distension.
But this is the extent of our judgment and skill
in making much out of little
or piercing the stone of enclosures.

Coltsfoot

Coltsfoot flourishes on shingly screes and dunes
and leaps forward on runners called stolons
like a messenger speeding from tower to city
with news to alert the defenders.
It is known as *Filius ante patrem*,
the son before the father,
for the advent of the flowers before the leaves.
It is rich in mucilage and tannin
and served as a decoction or syrup
it makes a lulling expectorant.
Combined with betony, eyebright, bogbean, deadnettle and
hawthorn
it yields an herbal tobacco
prescribed for catarrh of the lung as well as the hangover.
Fresh crushed leaves mixed with honey in a cataplasm
are anathema to varicose veins and suppurating wounds.
But when applied in advance of the defect
it works by anticipation of the sequel
to prevent the onset of the avoidable
and thus for those with an eye to the future
it is a veritable benediction.
Coltsfoot is indeed a lively and abounding plant
and amends the before that comes after
by the after that comes before
for the son is always the redemption of the father.

Herb Robert

Herb Robert is leafy, hairy and stenchy
with an erect red stem
that causes a maiden to blush.
The fruit resembles the beak of a crane
and was thus by the Greeks known as *gheranos*
but its common names derives from Latin *rubor*, or red
as ruddies the head of the male device
or the cheeks of the maiden in fear and delight.
Herb Robert stanches the haemorrhage
and is an incomparable wound herb
and an electuary for retention of milk in the breasts
but is most efficacious in melting resistance
by virtue of shock and the Doctrine of Signatures
to redden the sheet with compliance.

Butterbur

Butterbur grows in wet peaty meadows
and by marshy riverbanks and fenny swamps.
The leaves appear in April, after the flowers,
large and flat like a trowel or spatula.
The petals of the flowers are flesh-coloured or pale plum,
bell-shaped in the male and full of nectar,
thread-like in the female and without nectar,
and are followed by the white lanular pappus
which crowns the seed.
Its ancient name comes from Greek *petatos*,
shepherd's felt hat,
for the leaves may be used as a covering for the head,
but the common term "butterbur" is empiric
for the leaves are used to wrap butter in warm weather.
It is considered a capital medicine against the ague
and the powder of the roots
cures all naughty filthy lacerations and fistulas.
It is also good for pains of the back and the loins
in those who tumble off a bridge during a stroll
or pump too frequently upon the body of a woman.
Butterbur must be fathered with care
for once it seizes upon a plot of ground and takes hold
no other vegetation can live where it grows
under its canopy of leaves extinguishing light.
Butterbur is not to be trifled with
though its uses are many and kindly to man
and a boon in particular to lovers and cooks.

Hyssop

Hyssop is an holy herb
and comes from the Greek *azob*, the "sacred bush,"
and is spoken in the bible as a cleansing plant
for the psalmist chants
"Purge me with Hyssop and I shall be clean."
It is sometimes found wild on dry rocky slopes
and is cherished for ornament
with its long dense spikes and tubular flowers
and its many square and woody stems
primped and filamented roundabout the tops.
It is delicious when added to salads, game soups and fruit pies
and aids the digestion of greasy fats
and its oil is a grace in liqueurs of the monks
as it is in perfumes of elegant ladies.
Hyssop tea and balnearies are remedies for the rheumatik
but it should never be taken by a pregnant wife
for it is a clamant emmenagogue
and may prowl calamitous in the guts.
But this is a hapax legomenon
and in general gratuitous.
Hyssop grows merrily in an herb garden
and makes a pretty edging plant
as in yarking an embroidered tapestry
and England is the richer for my cultivating it.

𝕷𝖆𝖉𝖞'𝖘 𝕸𝖆𝖓𝖙𝖑𝖊

Lady's Mantle is known as *Alchemilla vulgaris*
for it is beloved of the common folk
who see in its proliferation an eidolon of themselves
as it is cherished by alchemists
for its many wondrous properties.
Lady's Mantle is native to damp grasslands, open woods
and rock-ledges in mountain fastnesses.
It has a stout black rootstock
and great denticle leaves clustered in rosettes
but without petals,
its only flaw and deprivation.
For to be without petals is to be
shorn and destitute indeed,
yet Lady's Mantle compensates
by progeniture and many-sidedness.
Michel de Maisonneuve in his princely *Etymology*
deposes that its common name
derives from the scalloped edges
of its lobed, camisole leaves.
But Brother Carmino di Caserta
in his dissenting *Florilegia* thinks otherwise
for Lady's Mantle is a handsel of *flammeolum*
purfled and ruched at the verges
and signifies the bashfulness of brides in concinnity.
It is also called Woman's Best Friend
for it is used as a vulnerary
to stanch the bleeding of wounds from domestic mishap
and prevent catamenial extravasation.
It heals lesions after parturition.
A weak decoction of Lady's Mantle

steeped in a bowl of sweetened grog
or stirred in a syllabub,
heated with a warm iron
and applied with circumspection
depilates the hairy embarrassments of the flesh,
curtails the dewlap
and smoothes the pleats and deckles of the skin
and therefore it is prized by ladies to a fault
and propagated with devotion.
When foraged by kine it yields milk additionally
and when mixed with wine
it stimulates the appetite of men in dalliance
to seek forgetfulness of labour
in remembrance of harvest.
It is commonly found in gardens
and betimes as an escape
wedged in old walls, quarries and sea-cliffs.
Rabbi Asa in his *Treatise*
writes of Lady's Mantle
that it is a major miracle of the Lord
and akin to the manna
for its marvellous ubiquity and its power of sustenance
in the desert of our wandering
and the valley of our common desolation.

Porcelain Berry

Like a single porcelain berry
arboreal with derivation
and linked to the outermost twig
of the porcelain berry vine in winter,
Bartolomaeus Porphyrius
remains whole and selfsame,
proof against frost of treacherous scintillations;
and braced by the late bloom of ancestry
against the weathers of deposition,
remains circumscribed and held fast
on the tine of genealogy.
Thus I persist
among scaled icicles in glacier-scented wind.
I cling to the branches of lineation.
I breathe cold in and warmth out
to sustain my pedigree.
And plumed with snow
I rejoice in this blue bead of royal blood
gemming the map of origins.
For the porcelain berry heralds inheritance.

𝔈𝔫𝔳𝔬𝔦: 𝔕𝔬𝔰𝔢𝔪𝔞𝔯𝔶

Rosemary comes from *ros marinus*,
dew of the sea,
for it loves salt spray of the sea
on which the voyager departs,
tremulous and frail,
on his journey into *mare incognitum*.
It was brought to us by the Romans
who were great travellers in their time
and were needful of amendment
for anaemia, asthma, insomnia, anxiety and nervous migraine
which ailments accompany
the peregrine on his wanderings
like lubber fiends to his discomfiture
and which by rosemary are chastened and forestalled.
And therefore, go my little book
with flitters of rosemary sprinkled upon you
to act as an ecphractic dust
ensuring prosperity and endurance
in the tempest of the interim,
to guide your crossing as with gimbal rings and rutters,
and to parry the catenary nullifidian.

Acknowledgements

An artisanal "special edition" pamphlet of ten experimental, unbound pages of herbal entries appeared with Montreal Books in 2008. This initial effort has over the years expanded into the current book-length volume. My thanks to Asa Boxer and Michael Harris for their friendly encouragement.

About the Author

David Solway's most recent volume of poetry prior to *The Herb Garden* is *Installations* (Signal Editions, 2015). A CD of his original songs, *Blood Guitar and Other Tales*, appeared in 2014; with his pianist wife Janice Fiamengo he is currently recording a second album, *The Book of Love*. Among his many prose works, *The Big Lie: On Terror, Antisemitism and Identity* (Lester, Mason and Begg/Random House, 2007/8), figured on *The Montreal Gazette's* non-fiction bestseller list. His latest prose volume is *Reflections on Music, Poetry & Politics* (Shomron Press, 2016). Winner of many awards and formerly poet-in-residence at Concordia University, Solway also writes for the major American political sites such as *PJ Media, FrontPage Magazine, American Thinker* and *WorldNetDaily*.